T0142616

MY JOURNEY BACK TO FREEDOM

Lauretta Bell

© 2019 Lauretta Bell. All rights reserved.

No part of this book may be reproduced, stored in a retrieval system, or transmitted by any means without the written permission of the author.

AuthorHouse™
1663 Liberty Drive
Bloomington, IN 47403
www.authorhouse.com
Phone: 1 (800) 839-8640

Because of the dynamic nature of the Internet, any web addresses or links contained in this book may have changed since publication and may no longer be valid. The views expressed in this work are solely those of the author and do not necessarily reflect the views of the publisher, and the publisher hereby disclaims any responsibility for them.

Any people depicted in stock imagery provided by Getty Images are models, and such images are being used for illustrative purposes only.
Certain stock imagery © Getty Images.

This book is printed on acid-free paper.

ISBN: 978-1-7283-3232-1 (sc)
ISBN: 978-1-7283-3231-4 (e)

Print information available on the last page.

Published by AuthorHouse 10/28/2019

authorHOUSE®

CONTENTS

ABOUT THE AUTHOR

My name is Lauretta Bell and my book would be helpful to those that consider life is over when you are down. You are actually just beginning again when you fall. I fell down and I got back up. It wasn't easy. I had to keep on going. I had a little family to take care of. Everybody told me I would not make it but look at me now. I received my General Education Development in 2008 and a degree in Criminal Justice in 2014. I want each and every individual at any age to know that it is never ever to late to make it. I consider myself extremely blessed. I didn't ask anyone for help. My future goal is to be securely successful. I want to continue to learn new things and to keep growing. I want to know and accept who I am. I am happy and so grateful that I could turn a negative to a positive. I am thankful for my past troubles because I learned how to take advantage of it. Its called self motivation. I am a strong, intelligent and persistent woman creating my dreams. I have come a long way just to get this far. I struggled for a long time to get where I am. I never gave up. It doesn't matter what you go through in life. You can't look back just keep moving forward. It will get better and you must believe it. Be thankful when you are tired and weary because it means you have made a difference. I would love for my grandchildren to know you never get to old to learn and that you do make a difference. Love yourself and GOD everyday.

CHAPTER 1

My name is Lauretta Bell Shine, and this is my story.

When I was a little girl, my father was a bad man and was very mean to my mother. As I can remember, my father beat my mother so badly that she was sick all the time. One day, she got tired of him beating her, so she left and went back home to her parents' house, bringing me with her. Some days later, he came to her mother's house, took me from my mother's arms, and said, "You will never see this gal again." Like a good mother, she went back home with my dad. When he got her home, he beat her like she was lower than a dog. I didn't think anyone could ever beat a human being like that.

My mother was better off dead than to keep taking the beatings he gave her. The beatings went on for some years. When I was about six or seven years old, they got in a bad fight. She was washing my hair, and that made him mad, so he slammed me to the floor and broke my left leg.

I had four brothers and four sisters. I don't know anything about them.

As the years went by, I began remembering some things. I could see things changing. I do remember my mother was short, and her hair was black and long. I know she loved red lipstick. My dad wouldn't buy her any, so she took the soot from the stovetop and made it herself. She loved blood-red lipstick.

Every time a child was born, my father would beat my mother. Even when she was pregnant, he still beat her.

If he had leftovers, like a bologna sandwich, he would eat over half of it and then give the rest to us.

My mother died in the arms of my father's future wife. They gave my mother all kinds of medicine to kill her. One day when I came home from school, an old man met me down the street and told me my mother was sick. Then, as I remember, the doctor told my father to take my mother straight to the hospital. The doctor said, "Do not stop off anywhere, and do not give her anything to eat or drink." But she drank a soda, and as soon as she swallowed it, she died.

Some weeks later, my father married the lady whose lap my mother had laid her head in. After he married her, he split us children up. Some of my brothers and sisters stayed with my aunt. He kept the ones who could stand up without falling so they could go to the field and pick cotton. That included me, my sisters Rebecca and Sarah, and my brother Nate.

My father and his new wife had a baby boy. Then my father started beating my stepmother and busted her head. Blood went everywhere.

He started having women over to the house, including his wife's friends. He would make her leave the house while he had sex with them. Then, if he thought she was looking at any man, he would beat her until he became tired. Then he would make her cook them food. She would cook, but she didn't give us anything to eat until he was finished eating. They had three more boys.

I was sleeping around with my daughter's father. Then my stepmother found out and told my father.

He started allowing women to come over, and he would make us go outdoors. We wanted to know why every time women came over, he would make us go outside. We started to peek in the window to see what he was doing. That went on for a long time.

Then he started to see a lady's little girl. He stopped seeing the mother to start seeing the daughter. Everything started looking fishy. When the little girl came over, he would close the door, and we would start peeking again. We still didn't know what was going on, but we got an eyeful when he put the girl's hand on his penis and rubbed it.

He would send home these girls, and they'd come back three to four days later. He told us to go get them for him. Then he raised their dresses up and rubbed his penis between their legs.

We still didn't know what he was doing until this boy asked me for sex, and I told him I didn't have any. He showed me what sex was. I thought, *I saw my daddy do this to those women and the little girls.* So I did it, and I was scared. And my first time, I got pregnant. Some months later, my family found out. I was sick for nine months and went through hell. I still picked cotton, chopped beans, cut corn, pulled cotton, slept on the floor, and picked broken glass off the ground while on my knees. Nine months went by.

One morning, my father called us to go to work. I couldn't get up. When they came in with an extension cord and pulled the covers back, I was bleeding like a hog but couldn't say anything but, "Cramp." I had my baby without a doctor and without medicine—or care, or a hospital, or a nurse. I made her, me and God. When I was carrying my baby, everybody wanted the baby to be born dead.

I found a black Bible somewhere and carried it for nine months under my left breast. I didn't know how to pray, but the Lord knew what I was trying to say every time I got on my knees. Then when I had my baby, my father told my stepmother that he didn't want her anymore. My stepmother's brother had a wife, and my father was going with my stepmother's brother's wife. My father plotted to leave my stepmother. He fixed up a big lie so my stepuncle would leave his wife. He made me go to my stepuncle's wife and tell her my baby was her husband's. My uncle left his wife, and that was all my father wanted. Then it was on. My father started going with my uncle's wife but still slept with my stepmother.

My dad's new girlfriend was nasty and unclean and couldn't cook, so when he was ready to eat, he would go over to my stepmother's house to eat.

I asked my stepmother, "Why would he have sex with little girls?" They were about seven to eight years old. He would bring them over to the house and play with them with his hands under their dresses. Then in a few minutes, he would bend them over and put his penis between their legs, and he played with their privates with his hand. When he was finished, he gave them a piece of candy and a nickel and sent them home to their mothers. Their mothers would come over two or three days later, and he would have sex with them.

Weeks went by, and my dad was still beating my stepmom. He beat me so much that I left home all the time. I would run through the cornfield so he couldn't find me, but then he started shooting through the cornfield to kill me. I didn't care. I got tired of him beating on us all the time for no reason.

We didn't go to school in the summertime because we had to work. Everyone called us dummies when we went to school. We went to school only in the wintertime. We had a big farm where we raised cows, pigs, goats, chickens, and turtles. I didn't have time to play. None of us kids played.

CHAPTER 2

When I was about twelve years old, I saw things a lot better and started watching things closely. When my dad was finished beating us, he would place a brick on the table and put about four to five tablespoons of water on a plate. He would place our hands on that brick and give us one hundred hits on the hands. If we moved our hands, we would get another one hundred hits. When our hands were hot, he told us to place them on that plate because he liked to see the water cool off our hands.

As more time passed, I began working at the cotton gin. My dad came home one day and was mad at someone at work. He told my stepmom to leave the house. He brought another woman over for sex, and then he told her to go home.

When I was older, I began seeing a boy I liked, and everyone kept calling me a slut. I didn't know what a slut was. One day, the boy came over and asked me for sex, but I told him I didn't have any and that if he could wait, I could ask my dad and stepmom if they had any. He said, "No, don't ask them because they might beat you."

I asked him, "Why would you ask me for something that could get me beat up?"

He said, "Please don't ask them, but one day I will show you that you do have it."

I said, "Okay, as long as you don't beat me."

"He said, "I won't hurt you."

Time passed, and my boyfriend finally showed me what he was talking about. It was sex. I didn't know what sex was because nobody told us about sex. Then I realized it was what my dad was doing to those little girls and the women who came over to the house. It was all about sex.

Time went on, and I worked seven days a week. My brothers and sisters were slaves and had no friends. We had cousins, but we weren't allowed to play with them because to them, we had a disease. Nobody liked us. We never had hugs from anyone, not even strangers on the street. We never had anyone to kiss us on the forehead or the cheek.

One night my boyfriend called me outside, and he showed me how to kiss. Three or four weeks went by, and then he showed me again. Then I saw what my father had done. My boyfriend and I did it—we had sex. After that, I was so sick I couldn't walk. I had to tell my dad I'd slipped, fallen, and hurt my legs on the truck. I never wanted that again, but about six weeks later I found out I was pregnant. When they found out, I went through pure hell. I still had to pick one hundred pounds of cotton every day, or he would beat me. I chopped corn and cut beans. I couldn't pick up the sack; I had to pull it. When I came home, he made me pick up broken glass. He didn't want me to be pregnant. When I was born, he'd wanted me to be a boy. This was why he'd treated my mother like he did, because I was a girl.

Now that he knew I was pregnant, he was really mean. He hung me up at the top of the ceiling with a rope around my neck. My hands were tied behind my back, and my feet were tied together. I stood on a chair, and he beat me with a double extension cord while I wore only panties and a bra. I was still pregnant and working. He put some welts on my back and said I would be able to show these to my great-great-grandkids.

My mother died in the arms of the woman my father later married. Then he spread us children around to live with his aunt and other family members. He and his second wife had a son. Everyone told her not to marry my father. She married him so the other women wouldn't get him. She saw him beat my mother, and then she married him. He started beating her. She had four children, and my stepmother and all her children were in the cotton field picking one hundred pounds of cotton a day. The children ranged in age from eight to twelve years at the time we had to work. We were so tired, but when we arrived home, he forced us to cut wood, pick up broken glass out of the yard, and wash baby diapers.

We had a brother who was ill, so we had to feed him every day. Sometimes we would still be hungry, so we would eat his food in order to have strength to pull the cotton sack the next day starting at 4:00 a.m. We would never get paid for the work. He would bring sandwiches to work, and he would eat over half the food before he gave us a bite. It was rude, but we would eat anyway because we were hungry.

When I was a little girl, my father was bad to my mother—I mean really bad. I can remember my father used to beat my mother so badly that she was sick all of the time. She got tired of him beating on her, so she left and went back home to her parents' house, taking me with her. Then he came to her mother's house, took me from my mother's arms, and said, "You will never see this girl again." Like a good mother, she went back with my father. When he brought her home, he beat her. My mother was a sweet mother. She would've been better off dead, given the beatings he gave to her. The beatings went on for some years. Then I had some more brother and sisters, four boys and four girls. My mother couldn't wear makeup, but she could wear red lipstick. When all the children were born, he started beating her again, and then he started going with other women. He found out that I could pick cotton, and when I was six years old, he made me and my mother pick cotton.

She pulled me on her cotton sack. She had to pick up to one hundred pounds of cotton per day before he was pleased. Two more of the children grew to be able to pick cotton. When my mother got sicker, he started leaving her at home and going with the lady next door. A woman and older man used to give my mother Prince Albert cigarettes. Before my father would come home, I would hide the cigarettes under the house so he wouldn't find her secret place. Then he would come home and would start something so he could have a good reason to beat her. She could not do anything. She would go into the next room so he wouldn't see her, get mad, and beat her to keep her from going outdoors. To keep her from going outside, he would put a twenty-five-gallon can in the bedroom so that she could use it for her bathroom. She could not go outdoors or to the bathroom unless he was with her. She could not take us out to play unless we sat on the porch corner.

When I was eight years old, my mother got sicker. My father was going with lots of women by then. When my dad went off with other women, they would come to see my mother when my dad was gone to get her something to make her well. Weeks later, another lady would come over and give her something that made her feel worse. When I went to school and came back home, this older gentleman who would help take care of my mother told me she was dying. I didn't understand what he was saying, and I did not believe him. They let her stay home another day, and then another lady came and told her to take some ashes, boil them in water, and drink it. She did and got sicker. Then they called Dr. Holiefield, and he came to check on her. He told my dad to take her to Memphis to the nearest hospital and to not stop anywhere no matter what. They all got into the car, and as they were driving, lo and behold, they stopped at a store to get her something to drink. They ignored the doctor's orders to not give her anything to eat or drink. They gave her something to drink, and she died before she arrived at the hospital.

When I was fifteen years old, I met Mr. Shine. We grew up together, played together, went to school together, and worked together. One day he asked me for sex. I was a young girl and didn't know what that was. He asked me to come over, and I did so about a month later. He showed me what sex was, and like a little girl, I went with him that night, doing what he asked. I gave myself to him every time he asked me for sex. My dad found out I was having sex, and he almost killed me. But I had seen him having sex with other little girls. I did not know what he was doing with them. I kept on doing it until I got pregnant. I knew if my dad found out, he would kill me. I got a beating day and night. I was sixteen years old, and I kept leaving, but he kept looking for me. When he found me, he would beat me, so I would leave home again. He started shooting at me because I had a boyfriend.

My boyfriend was not helping me. I had a baby girl and had to find rags on the ground and in the mud to dress her. I would wash them for my baby and sew her clothing.

My dad was so mean and evil and had his way with people. He would beat up other people because he could, and nobody would do anything about it. He would take the money from his own children so that he could buy other women dresses, shoes, pants, blouses, food, and makeup. He would also drive them around in new cars that he bought. The money that we had was from picking cotton. He would give our money to the pretty girls, treating us like we were ugly. No one liked us, not even our own cousins, who were treated better than us. He started having sex with young girls and their mothers. He would bring the girls over to the house, and he would put his hands on them and between their legs. He played with their hands and made those girls do all kinds of things. We didn't know what he was doing to the girls. When he was done with them, he would send them home. The next day, he would have sex with these girls who were so young—third and fourth graders. He would bring them over to our house and put his hands under their dress. A few moments later, he would bend them over and put his hands between their legs. When he was finished, he would give them some candy and money and send them home to their mother. Then the mothers would come over, and he would have sex with them.

As the weeks went by, he kept beating both me and my stepmom. He beat me so much that I left, running through the cornfields because he was trying to kill me. I did not care because I was tired of him beating on us all the time for no reason. He's was a mean man.

We were only allowed to go to school in the winter. We did not go to school in the summer. We always had to work, and the other children called us dummies when went to school. We had a huge farm that raised cows, pigs, goats, chickens, and turkeys, so none of the children had time to play.

I think I was about twelve years old when I began to see things a lot clearer. I started listening and watching closer. He would whip us and wait until it rained. He would have a good reason to be at home so he could think of something that would bring us a lot of pain. He had us to put some water into a plate and put our hands in hot water. Then he liked to see cool water run over our hands. This was painful.

I started working at the cotton gin. My dad came home and got mad at someone at work, and he told my stepmom to leave the house. He had another woman over to have sex, and then he told her to go home. If he thought my stepmom was looking at another man, he would beat her. He made my stepmom cook his food. When she did cook for him, she did not give us anything to eat until he was finished eating. He would beat her until he was tired.

I was older now and seeing a boy I liked. Everybody called me a slut, but I didn't know what that meant. A woman who would lay down with a thing like a dog? One day he came over and asked me for sex. I asked him, "What is that? I don't have any. You can wait, and I can ask my mom and dad if they have sex."

He said, "No, don't ask them that. If you ask them that, they might beat you."

I asked him, "Why would you ask me for something to get me beat?"

He said, "Please don't ask them. One day I will show you. I have a place for us to have sex."

I said, "As long as you don't beat me."

He said, "I will not hurt you."

Time passed, and then my boyfriend showed me what he was saying. It was sex. No one had told me about sex. I had not been told about sex; my mother was dead, so who would tell me about it? I then knew what my dad was doing to all those girls and women who were coming over to our house. Time went on, and I worked seven days a week. My siblings and I were slaves. We had friends, but they weren't allowed to play with us because we had to work day and night.

The beatings were not effective anymore, so he would tie my feet and my hands behind me, hang my up by my neck while standing on a chair, and beat me until he was satisfied. I had open-wound slashes and welts on my back, and blood was everywhere. For two or three weeks, while my back was trying to heal, he would beat me to open the flesh back up. My back was still raw, but that did not stop him. The next day, I went to work and had to pull one hundred pounds of cotton. I went to work, and people saw blood oozing through my shirt. While I pulled cotton, nobody asked me what had happened. They knew that if they did, he would beat me again.

While I was pregnant, he tried to kill my baby by beating me. My stepmother was pregnant with her ninth child, so he beat both of us. Three months went by, and we were in bed one night after working the day before. The next morning, around three or four, it was time for us to get up and go to work. He called for everybody to get up for work, and they did. I did not get up; I did not say anything because he had that extension cord in his hand. If I said something, he may hit me, and I may lose my baby. I let him do what he wanted. He pulled back the covers, and my baby's head was showing. I had her in the back room all alone, just me and God. I didn't know who God even was. They cut the cord. I never saw a doctor the entire nine months that I was carrying my baby.

I never had one pill for pain. I was bleeding so badly that I didn't say a word. I was cramping bad. No medicine. No hospital care. No nurse. I simply had my baby girl. Like I said, I did not know who God is, but I was so glad that he was there. My doctor was God.

When I was pregnant with my daughter, my dad and my stepmom did not want me to have my baby. They wished my baby was born dead. One day I had ran up to an older lady. She gave me a Bible and told me to carry it under my left breast. I didn't know how to pray, but the Lord knew what I needed and what I was trying to say every time I got down on my knees.

My dad told my stepmom he no longer needed her anymore. My stepmom didn't leave. She had a brother who did not work. My dad told me to tell my stepmom that my baby was his. Then she would leave, and he could start sleeping with her brother's wife. He had me go tell my uncle's wife that my baby was her husband's. It was a big lie to get my uncle's wife to leave. She knew who my baby's father was—everyone knew—but he still broke apart that family. He still went over to my stepmom's because she could cook.

I asked my stepmom why she allowed him to beat her like that, and she said because she loved him. I told her, "He doesn't love you. He hates women. Why don't you leave him? You saw what he did to my mother. You saw what he did to you while you were pregnant. He dragged you downstairs. And you know about the other women he brings to the house. You saw what he did my mother, but you still married him. He tells you after we are older that he doesn't need you. He didn't want you in the first place. Now he is going to kill you, just like my killed my mother. And you say you love him? He never loved you at all. He simply used you. There is love anywhere in his heart. He is just waiting for us to be grown."

I was still slipping around with my boyfriend (my baby's father). We got caught kissing. My dad acted like I'd killed a police officer. Oh, my gosh! He called me in the house and tied me up. He put string around my mouth and stood me in a corner with a cord around my neck. When he beat me, he knew if I slipped, I would hang myself.

He had life insurance on me, so he knew he would have all that money. He could spend it on other young women. He beat me until blood came from every part of my body. He beat me so badly that I could not cry anymore. He kept beating until I was numb and felt no pain. I had no feeling in my body at all. Blood dripped everywhere. He beat me so badly that I ran away from home and went inside a nickel-and-dime store. I stole a spool of thread so that I could go to jail. All of that for kissing my boyfriend. I was sick all night. I tried to think how I could get the money he had in his pocket so I could leave. I knew that if I got that money, it was not his. My sister and brother had made that money. Now I knew that if I got that money, I was going to die. And where would I go? I never went anywhere except to work. I took the money anyway.

The next morning, he noticed the money was missing. He was going to beat everyone in the house because he knew I had the money. To keep him from telling the other children I had the money, he had everyone empty their pockets. No one had it because I had hidden it in the outhouse next door. I begged God to help me because I couldn't go home. I gave up the money because I didn't want him to beat my other sisters and brothers. He beat me again two days later. After that beating, I was still in pain and sore days later. I had to go back to work and pull sacks of cotton. For lunch, I had one-third of a sandwich and one drop of a soda pop. I had enough water to wet my tongue. Each and every time that man came home, we would be so scared. We didn't know who he was going to beat next. I was so afraid. Every time I saw my dad, I had anxiety and was nervous. I thought I was going to get a beating every time he saw me because I had taken the money.

One day, I dropped my baby on the side of the stove, and she got burned on the side of her head. It took some time for her hair to grow back. This was how afraid I was: whenever I saw him, I dropped my baby. I was so tired of my dad beating me.

No one ever said anything about my mother—when she died, where she was buried, what she was like. I asked my dad, and he didn't say anything. I did not understand. My dad did not drink or do drugs. He was simply a mean man. We were scared of him. I know a lot of people were scared of him.

I got married to my boyfriend on August 24, 1968. My daughter was born on May 3, 1964. I was glad to get married. I left the cotton field. I got married so I wouldn't have to receive any more beatings. I left my sisters and brothers. I did not want to, but I had a husband. We were at work, so when we got off, we got married. We got off work at 11:00 a.m. and went to the courthouse. It took us about fifteen minutes. We did not kiss, and we went back to work. He drove a tractor. We would plant corn and soybeans. I picked cotton.

When we came home that night, we went to sleep, sleeping on the floor. We had to put cotton in a sack while working all day. The cotton sack was what we covered up with to sleep. That was all that we had. It was a nasty bag, but I wasn't getting any more beatings. We would leave some cotton in the bag so we could have a pillow at night. It felt good to me, but he wasn't raised like this. He'd had a bed, blankets, and food. I was not used to his style, and he was not used to mine.

We worked for a while and walked to work. We walked when we had to get groceries. We bought new sheets, pillowcases, and a wood stove for me to cook our food. That was our two-week anniversary. We slept like this until we found an old house in a field. The house did not belong to anyone, and we had to stay somewhere. No one wanted to help us. The house had no windows and no furniture. We had no clothes, no blankets, no bed, and no food. There was no one to help us. We had no car. We had to walk to the store.

A year after we were married, he started having sexual relations with other women, like my dad did. I didn't know what was going on. I was sick every time I caught him with other women. Every week, I thought I was going crazy. I would see him in cars having sex with other women.

My sister was one of those women. That hurt me so bad. My dad had sex with everyone. I married this man, and his cheating went on for two years. Then his cousin came to town and asked us to stay with them. My husband could get a job with him. We went because I knew that would be good for us. About two months after the move—I really don't know how long we were there—my husband sent me to Chicago to see if I liked it there at his cousin's house. For about a week and a half, I liked the city. There were pretty cars, homes, apartments, and grocery stores, and lots of factory work. I went back home and told my husband I liked it. He said, "We have to think about it for a minute." I said okay. It sounded good and looked good. We got our paycheck and got on the bus. Chicago, here we come! I was the happiest woman in the world. I had my husband to myself, and I didn't have to think about those other women. I left my life behind.

My new life was just getting started while staying with his cousin. There were too many children, though—they had twelve in that house at the time. We had nowhere else to go, so we stayed with them for about two and a half months. We saved up enough money to get our own apartment. Time went on, and soon we bought all kinds of furniture I had never seen. Our bed was so soft that he was late to work for about a week due to sleeping so soundly. We were not used to having a bed with a mattress. When I was at home, I would sleep on a spring with a sack for a sheet. I didn't have to work. My husband was no good, but he took care of me for a while.

He ran into some city women. I was dumb as a bat, and I didn't know anything about men, including my husband. As time went by, everything happened fast. I decided I was going to fight for my husband. His cousin's wife started going with my husband. She also started borrowing money and had no job to pay it back. We tried to buy a home. He had a job working for Quaker Oats. The company gave him the money to get a home.

I sat around all day long, waiting. He cashed the check and had no money when he finally got home. All the money was spent. We had no money and no home. He made up his mind that he was leaving me. For one and a half years, he kept coming back. I let him back in; this was 1972. The Quaker Oats Company gave him back his job. We put the money back up. He then started gambling. Every weekend he was gambling with somebody. Then he stopped paying and buying food. My baby and I had no food every night. I would go and find him just so he could buy some food.

There was a man who always liked me, so I started acting like a city girl. What I was going to do was wrong, but I had to feed my baby. I said to myself, *I must do this for her.* I said to the man, "This is my first time doing this."

He said, "It's not good. I can't do you this way. I tell you what I will do. Every time your husband comes down here and I win his money, I will give his money to you so you can pay your bills and buy food. Stop running behind him like that because you are not a little girl. Don't let him see you doing that."

That man who was giving me the money wasn't lying: my husband was no good. He was trying to mess with his own daughter. She was afraid of him, but she did not want to tell me because he'd told her not to. He said, "If you tell your mother, I will kill both of you."

She said to me, "I will take care of you, not him. He doesn't have money, a car, or a place to stay. So I must take care of you like my dad, and I will always take care of myself."

I was looking for love. I didn't know what love was until I was thirty years old. It wasn't what I thought it was. I started going with this man, who was a truck driver. He started taking me out to dinner. I never knew what it was like to eat at fine restaurants. I was so happy that this man had started off treating me like this. In due time, he changed his behavior. I had some furniture in layaway, and he helped me to get it out. Then one weekend, my sister and I went out, and he couldn't find me.

When we got home, this man had cut up all my furniture. Then he started going with other women. I said, "What is my problem here?" I hadn't learned anything. We fought every night for nothing. I would not get any sleep, so he started taking me on the road so he could keep tabs on me at all times. He never kept a job and tried to find out where I was. I started driving school buses. I drove buses for twelve years. I loved my job because I felt free from everyone.

The beatings went on for years. I was still trying to keep my daughter in school. I was a single mom trying to make it with no help from anyone. I got beat when I was at home as a child all my life. Then I was beaten by a man I thought was good. I was no city girl. I was not looking for a man. I was simply trying to make it. It was hard. I am so glad God gave me one child, and I really do love my daughter. I did not think we were going to make it. I still have pain in my back today from all the beatings. One day, those beatings I endured are going to pay off. I don't know when, but I will be glad when that day comes.

He calls me to come to Dallas. I came and helped him. I taught him how to buy food and make ends meet. He did not know love. I stayed three days, but Dallas was too fast for me. I went back to Chicago. I thought I was home for good. There I went again, this time in an airplane on my way back to Dallas. I stayed three more days, but he had another woman. Back to Chicago I went. Money was getting low, so I got my daughter and granddaughter, and we put everything we could in my car and drove to Texas, this time to stay permanently. This was this biggest mistake I have ever made. We were in Texas for a month, and this man acted like he didn't know who we were. I was so ashamed. Now I had nowhere to go with my girls. I remember that my dad used to tell us to keep at least one hundred dollars because you can never tell when you will have to run.

That was no lie. I didn't have to run, but I learned how to save money. It lasted us about a year. Two to three weeks after that, he put us out when the money ran out, and we had nowhere to go. I had a car that we would sleep in, but I had to ride until I could find us a safe place to rest. This went on for two years. We didn't know anyone in Dallas. I was not looking for anyone to help us. Nobody had ever helped, so why should I look for help now? I was going to do the best I could. I had to save my kids. Every day, we would ride out in Kiest Park so he could not find us. Whenever we got a chance, we went to the grocery store so we could get some air-conditioning because it was so hot. Sometimes we would go to McDonald's, Burger King, or Kentucky Fried Chicken so that we could freshen up. We would do that every morning to wash ourselves and to give the baby a bath.

Eventually we started looking for help and any type of assistance. The places we went asked for all kinds of documents with addresses. I did not have any of that—not one thing with an address. "We cannot help you without those things," they said. I tried for hours but received no help and no food, so we went back to the park for a few days. After we had rested, we found a grocery cart and took it. We found some rags, put them in the cart, and rolled the baby in it. We started taking turns pushing each other. We found two more carts took those too. This was what we started sleeping in every night. It was tight, but we made it work. The following days, we would roll until we found a place like a restaurant where we could clean up. We were happy that we had a place to sleep.

We found a grocery store so we could get a load of bread. It was one dollar per loaf. Bologna sold for sixty cents, and we'd buy a one-liter soda. I would buy this to last us for two days because we didn't have a refrigerator or a freezer. I would put the food in storage bags or the grocery store bag and hide it in a deep hole in the ground. I would mark it so I could find it when we were ready to eat again. This went on for a year.

I thought I would like to drive trucks, so I decided to try. I started driving the school bus. I got hired and thought that we could sleep some nights on my bus. I still did not have an address. One day while rolling down the street in Oak Cliff, a lady said, "I have been watching you with those kids. Where do you stay, momma?"

I said, "I don't have anywhere to stay, miss. This is where we stay, in this grocery cart. I am from Chicago, and I don't know anyone here."

She said, "Come with me," and we did. She took us to this apartment with one bedroom and told me we could stay until we were doing better. For a while, we started feeling good. We could take baths and brush our teeth. We could run all over the house and play, and we could go get the food that we had hidden in the hole.

After my boyfriend put us out, I hadn't seen him for about six months. He found where we were living. When he came over, I refused to open that door. He kicked it in because he thought I had a man inside. I said, "This lady is going to put us out. I can't fix that door." We stayed until she came to check on us and to bring us some good food. When she saw the door was knocked down, she immediately asked for the keys. I was so mad. We had nowhere to go again. I was glad that we still held on to those grocery carts.

Here came my boyfriend riding around, humiliating us, riding in a Cadillac, and talking about us like we were nobody. After he was finished having his fun, he came back, and we had to stay with him. I really didn't want to, but I didn't have a choice. I was tired of walking. I thank God no one tried to hurt us. We didn't get sick, and the baby didn't get sick. When we went back, things didn't improve. The baby couldn't go outside. We couldn't use the bathroom, and we couldn't eat his food. We couldn't talk to other people. He was the apartment manager. He could've let us stay in an apartment with no pay. I thought I was his girlfriend. I guess not. I was simply a guest.

I think we stayed there for three days after he had broken down the woman's door before he put us out again. We had nowhere to go, so we went back to the park and tried to find something to eat. We didn't have any toilet paper, so we had to use leaves from the trees or grass. One day we were walking, and I saw this old hotel. I decided to see whether they were hiring. The lady hired me to housekeep rooms. Now I was in the door, and somebody in Texas knew me. I had to work this situation and find out how to sleep there. I got the job, and two days went by. I thought, *Okay, when I find out something, we can sleep in the hotel room every day.* I went to work at 9:00 a.m. every day, and I would find out how to switch. I would let my daughter and granddaughter come in the room while I cleaned. I would let them get under the bed and sleep while I cleaned all eighteen rooms. I did that for about a month. My daughter got hired to do the same work. When the office closed, we would leave one room undone.

When we received our first paycheck, we went to Kentucky Fried Chicken and ordered a bucket of chicken. We ate that whole bucket of chicken. Folks stared at us. They didn't understand what we had been through. We had not eaten cooked food in two years. I had promised them that when we got a paycheck, we were going to eat until we were full, and we did just that.

I got my old job back driving for the school bus. My daughter signed up for government aid. While the challenges were going on, this man was still fighting with me every few days. I was with someone new, and we would argue everyday too. I still was trying to take care of my girls. My daughter was seventeen and was trying to get an apartment. I worked for UPS here and there. I went to work. I was sick—not physically but mentally tired. My soul was sick. I was sick of having nowhere to go and nowhere to sleep. I was not clean, and we were smelly. My daughter got pregnant. I know she was not trying to, but things happen. We were still working but had no place to live.

One day I went to get my bus. I picked up all my children and was on my regular route, No. 66. I went across the Hampton Bridge. As I went across, the bus stopped. The keys were in the switch. I did not drive that bus. I knew it was God that day. I called the bus terminal and told them to come pick up the kids and bring a driver because this was my last time driving the bus. They called the paramedics to take me to the hospital. I was there three to four hours. The doctor came and told us I'd had a nervous breakdown. I could not drive the school bus anymore.

We went back to his house and remained there for one week. He put us out on Mother's Day. Now where were we going to sleep? I had some money saved up, but I was trying to keep it so that we would have a place to stay. He said we could not stay with him. I saw an apartment that I was able to rent for fifty dollars a week. I had to do this. My dad told me, "Lauretta, you'd better take care of those girls." I would have done anything, but I was not going to lie on my back. I didn't know how I was going to take care of them, but I was determined to do it. The rental house's old trailers were full of insects that were eating us up. They were bedbugs. We had to stay two more days. On the fifth day, we received a letter from Dallas Housing that my daughter could come pick up her voucher for the projects. We didn't know what that was. We found out it was an apartment. We were ready. We could take a bath or a shower! We went along without furniture, but that was okay. I found out that you must have three things in order to get on your feet in Dallas: a car, a phone, and a job. We were glad we didn't have to stay with other people.

He found out where we lived and was soon at the door. We let him in so that he would not break down the door again. Everyone was asleep. No man was in the apartment. I said, "I don't have time for you, so why would I have time for a man in my life when I have to take care of my girls?"

UPS was a part-time job. My daughter and I got jobs at the Marriott Hotel. I saved up to get us a car. I did not know we could go places and take the baby to the lake. Life went on, and I had not seen him for another six months. One day, he saw me and the girls as we went into the store in my car, a hatchback. It was mine. We were driving, and he saw us in the car. He said the car belonged to another man. He did not bother us for a few weeks. I guess he thought, *Where did she get that car?*

One morning, we were on the way out the door to work. The car would not start. I looked under the hood. He had pulled all of the wires out of my car. He pulled them out and threw them over the fence. I knew I couldn't miss work—I had just gotten this job. What could I do to get us to work? I recalled what my husband had said. He told me when we were together, "Lauretta, every time I work on this car, I want you to watch me."

"For what?" I'd asked.

He'd said, "Because you might be by yourself someday, and you must know how to fix your car like I do." I was mad, and it was cold. I jumped the fence and got the wires. I figured it out by putting one wire here and another wire there. When I was finished, we putt-putted all the way to work. I had to fix the car because we didn't have anyone to keep the baby. In the parking lot, when we had a chance, we took turns checking in on her. We took our breaks at the same time to spend time with the baby. In those days, I'd never heard of anybody dying in the car. God was taking care of us. My daughter's baby was not even six weeks old. We went out to help him because we still didn't have the money to buy diapers or food. We worked for two weeks, and the boss didn't pay.

My boyfriend had a company of his own, so we worked for him. He didn't give us half of the pay in the next three days, as he said he would. I had to pay taxes. My daughter was still bleeding, so he took us to work. Then he went and laid up with other women while we worked and made money for him. I was still working at the Marriott. This was our time to start living. I had been outside for a long time. I would not let anyone put us out again. I refused.

If anyone looks in this book and sees herself, don't let your story not be told. You will help out the next woman who needs to tell her story. Don't look at the pretty books. Look inside yourself. When you have pain from long ago, put it in a book and help yourself get rid of that old pain, that brokenness and the long, painful hurt that tries to keep you down. I did it, and so can you. It is never over. Be thankful that you don't already have everything you desire. If you did, what would there be to look forward to? Be thankful that you don't know something because it gives you the opportunity to learn. Be thankful for the difficult times because they will allow you to grow. Be thankful for the opportunities that limitations give you. I am proof. Be thankful for new challenges; they will build your strength and character. Be thankful for your mistakes; they will teach you valuable lessons. Be thankful when you are tired and weary, because it means you have made a difference. It is easy to be thankful for the good things. A life of rich fulfillment comes to those who are thankful for setbacks. Find a way to be thankful for your troubles, and they can become your blessings.

I am a strong, intelligent, persistent lady creating my own dreams. I take personal responsibility for all of the information, skills, and learning necessary for my life to conceive my goals and dreams. I learned valuable lessons from every experience I have lived. I have self-motivation once I accept responsibility for creating my own life. I must choose the kind of life I want to create. I chose the kind of life where I create outcomes and experience worldly success. It is meaningless if I am unhappy. I must create the quality and peace of mind with God's help. I pray not because I need something but because I have a lot to thank God for.

When life knocks you down on your knees, it is the perfect position to pray. Don't mix bad words with your bad moods; you will never replace the words you speak. You don't control who works into your life, but you can control which ones you throw out. A mother thinks about her children day and night even if they are not with her. A mother loves her children in a way they will never understand. Life is what we make it. A bad attitude is like a flat tire. You can't go anywhere unless you change that tire. Try not to take things personally. What people say about you is actually a reflection of themselves, not you. You are much stronger than you think.

I have been walked on, used, and forgotten. I don't regret one moment. In those extraordinary moments, I have learned about people, friends, and family—who I can and cannot trust. Some people lie, and some are sincere. I have learned how to be myself and appreciate that I have some nice people in my life. I wish I had a mother who I could make laugh. When I cry, I wish she could wipe my tears and give me a hug and a kiss. She is no longer here for me. This is why my life was so hard. However, I made it. I am fifty years old. I got my GED in 2008. I went to Tyler Junior College and received my criminal justice degree. If you want nothing, you get nothing.

I needed Jesus in my life. I did not know him, but I do now. He is the teacher I had back then. He was my mother when she passed away. And he was my dad. God sent me to a place where I could learn all about Him. I don't know what the future holds for my life. I am intelligent enough to know that there is a God who lifts me up when I am down. When I am full, he carries me. When I was lost, God knew all about me. When I can't find my way, he will direct my path. He is my everything. I was a truck driver and a school bus driver. My life was and is such a blessing. I have come a long, long way. After all the things that I have been through, I did not think I would be here today. But look at me now. God has loved me, and now I can love myself truly. I am Lauretta Bell.

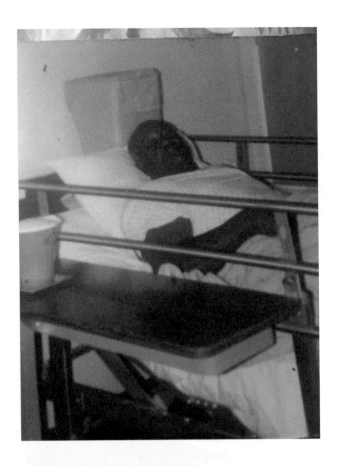

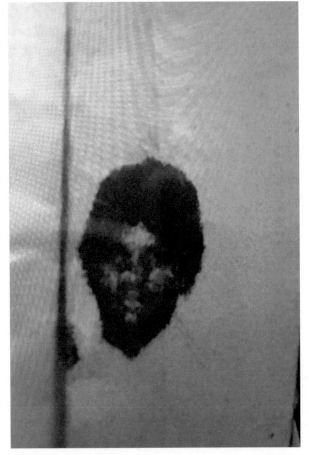

Lauretta Bell

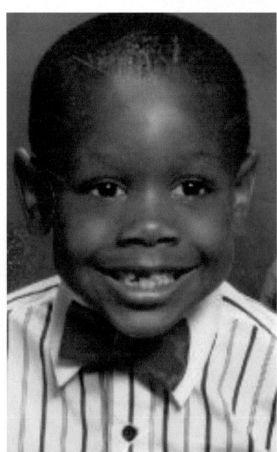

Printed in the United States
by Baker & Taylor Publisher Services